Forever
ON A
SWISS
MOUNTAIN

HOW 108 LIVES ENDED FOREVER ON A SWISS MOUNTAIN

Vol II

STEPHEN BLOOM

Author's introduction

If you look up on the internet the accident that befell Invicta 435 on 10th April 1973 at Basle, you will find very little information. Not so other accidents involving aeroplanes. Look up the Mount Erabus accident in Antarctica, or the mid-air collision over Zagreb, or the Staines air crash. You'll find dedicated books, if you're interested like me. But others are strangely absent. Where is a really good, dedicated book on the Tenerife collision of 1977, where 583 people died? Or the Dan Air crash of 1980 (*see my Vol I this series*).

Perhaps I'll take up writing about some of those other accidents soon? But of Invicta 435 – very little information! This particular accident was blamed upon the flight crew by the Swiss investigating authorities – the *Swiss Federal Department of Transport and Power*, who found that the accident was due mainly to a 'loss of orientation during two ILS approaches carried out under instrument conditions.' We will see later who was right.

Because aircraft accidents are nearly always a case of blaming someone – nobody, it seems, wants to take responsibility for what happens. The Dutch, for example, tried their upmost to wriggle out of responsibility for the Tenerife ground collision in 1977, in which 583 lives were lost (no disrespect to the Dutch). Yet, from the Spanish report, and air traffic tapes, it is obvious that KLM Captain Jacob Louis Veldhuyzen van Zanten, the chief KLM flying instructor of all people, clearly commenced his take off run in the belief that a Pan Am 747 had vacated the runway – and without a takeoff clearance from air traffic control, despite the American crew warning air traffic that they were still taxying down the foggy runway.

The French, as another example and the operator of Basle airport in 1973, tried in the Swiss report to blame the loss of 108 lives entirely upon the British flight crew – despite their air traffic controller, during a snow storm, not bothering to check the radar scope for the true location of Invicta 435, which had been driven off course by illegal radio transmissions that affected navigational instruments on board the Vanguard aircraft.

Believe me, I'm no expert in the field: no accident investigator nor pilot – in fact, I have just a passing interest in all things flying and flight simulation of the PC type – plus, I used to work in air traffic control during my days in the RAF at the London air traffic control centre (LATCC MIL) West Drayton in the early 1980's. But I feel that a fresh mind, looking over what evidence there is still available, can sometimes turn up new clues as to what happened.

Invicta 435 here will be my latest effort; perhaps the Tenerife ground collision and the Dan Air 1903 crash with another Spanish mountain might follow in my portfolio. I hope things may be clearer, by the end of this book, as to what happened in 1973, why it happened, and not be just another blame game between Britain, France and the Swiss. *This book is dedicated to all those who died, and their relatives.*

-Stephen Bloom 2017-

1

A shopping excursion to Basle!

That is all it was – a spring shopping trip to Switzerland – although it had become unseasonably cold suddenly in Europe that day, with snow falling in places, including Basle. This accident can be confusing, because of the various operating authorities involved. The destination airport, Basle/Mulhouse, is in France and controlled by French air traffic controllers. The town, Basle, is in Switzerland. The aircraft involved, Invicta 435, took off from the UK and was British registered, and it crashed at the hamlet of Hochwald/Solothurn, in Switzerland.

The actual aircraft involved – G-AXOP – of Invicta International, in which 108 people died and 37 survived (courtesy of R Vandervord)

The passengers were mainly women and children, for this was to be the third annual outing for members of the Axbridge ladies' guild, with the addition, on this occasion, of women from the Cheddar mums' night out group, and skittles players from Wrington and Congresbury – these places are all in Somerset. It was Tuesday 10th April 1973 when the happy travelers gathered at Bristol Lulsgate airport for their flight.

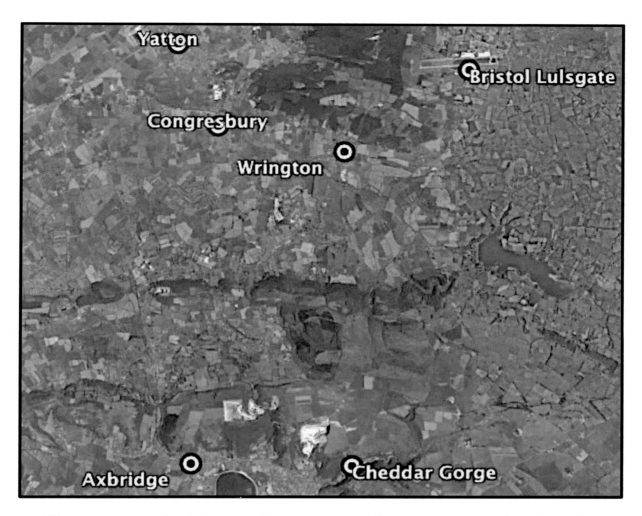

The towns and villages where most of the passengers lived – also Bristol Lulsgate airport where they took off from on the fateful day (courtesy Google Earth)

The aircraft was a British built Vickers Vanguard 952, operated by charter company Invicta International Airlines of Ramsgate, Kent – registration number G-AXOP. The aircraft was built in 1962, so was 11 years old at the time of the tragedy. Oscar Papa was equipped with four Rolls Royce 'Tyne 512' turbo-prop engines, each with a shaft horse-power of 5050; all engines had De Havilland built four blade constant speed propellers.

In an age of jets, this was not going to be a speedy flight to Basle; nor would it be particularly high in altitude. Our details from here regarding the flight to Basle and the accident derive mainly from the Swiss accident report, the ATC (Air Traffic Control) tapes and the aircraft FDR (Flight Data Recorder); the reason being there was no

CVR (Cockpit Voice Recorder) installed on the Vanguard, since it was not required by law at the time, which is a pity.

A photograph retrieved from a passenger's camera shows the passengers boarding ill-fated Oscar Papa at Bristol (unknown)

On board the 59027 kg aircraft to greet the passengers were four cabin crew: Gillian Manning (31), Joy Sadler (20), Elizabeth Low (26) and Daphne Axten (20). In the cockpit sat the two men who would fly them to Basle and back again the same day: Captain Anthony Noel Dorman (35), and Captain Ivor William Francis Terry (47). There was no flight engineer (FE) nor was one required.

With passengers on board, the Vanguard taxied and took off from Bristol Lulsgate airport at 07:19 in the morning. The flight to Basle was uneventful except for one important incident, that may have been a precursor of things to come. Tracked by French military radar, an unreported deviation from the middle of the airway between the Rolampont VOR (VHF Omni Range) beacon and the Luxeuil VOR navaids was detected. The aircraft was 10 NMs (Nautical Miles) south of the airway centre line, therefore 5 NMs outside of the airway.

Vanguard cockpit – co-pilot's side (thanks to Air team images)

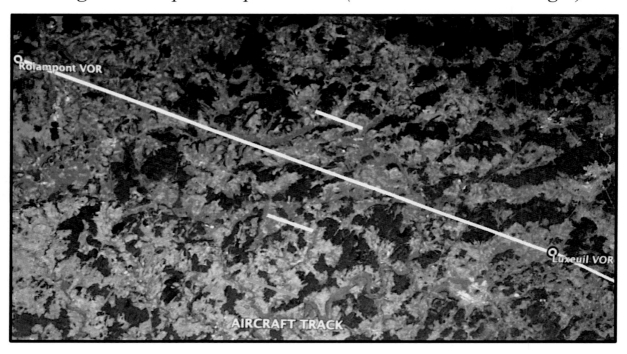

Problem between Rolampont VOR and Luxeuil VOR? Oscar Papa was tracked off course to the south (red marker approx.), 5 NMs from the airway edges (short white lines) (courtesy Google Earth)

Now there are several reasons why the Vanguard could have strayed from its course, the most obvious being strong winds blowing the aircraft off course. However, as part of even basic private pilot training, correcting your course to take into account strong winds causing drift becomes second nature. A strong, northerly blowing wind would drift Oscar Papa to the south, and out of the airway where she should have been. Only a failure of the pilot flying to navigate precisely could account for it.

Yet there were two experienced captains on board. If the wind was blowing from a north-east direction, the pilot would have to turn the nose of the aircraft towards it by a few degrees and 'crab' along the airway to maintain course. It could also, of course, have been a temporary mechanical failure of navigation equipment that caused the error during this time – as we shall see later, faulty equipment was discovered amongst the wreckage.

I'm not convinced this navigation drift was due just to pilot error, as we shall see later. It is necessary, however, to describe now the navigation equipment (of the time) involved in this tragedy. Firstly, there was the navaid VOR; this stands for VHF Omni Range. These were introduced in the time of high flying/high speed jets – the principle of operation is fairly simple. The VOR transmits two signals at the same time; one signal is constant in all directions and the other rotates about the station. Airborne equipment receives both the signals, electronically seeks the difference between them and interprets the result, which is a radial to or from the station.

Oscar Papa was equipped with two VOR receivers. The navaid is very good for precise navigation, because it is typically an 'upside down' cone shape, with the point at the ground transmitter. This means however, it is less useful for low level navigation, until almost upon the aircraft – especially in hilly or mountainous regions. Less in use today, but far more common in the 1950s/60s/70s is NDB/ADF, or Non Directional Beacon/Automatic Direction Finder. These beacons transmit on different frequencies to VOR, but are more so affected by earth curvature and most importantly, the weather.

Oscar Papa was equipped with two ADF receivers, to read NDB transmissions. They were part of the approach procedure to land at Basle Mulhouse airport, along with an instrument landing system (ILS) and various 'marker' locator beacons (inner marker IM, middle marker MM and outer marker OM).

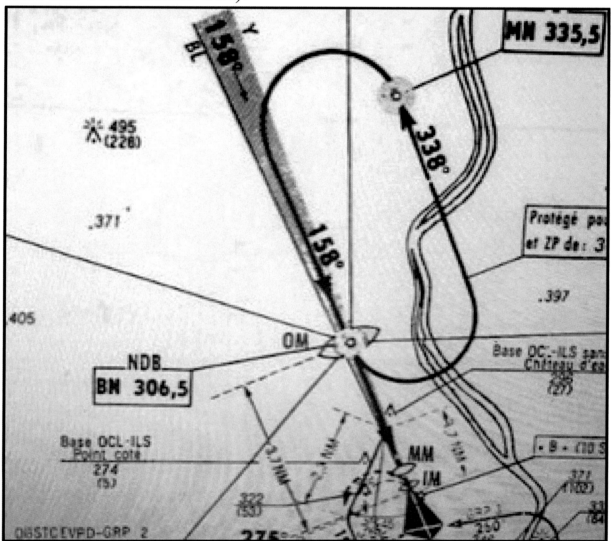

Basle/Mulhouse approach plate – looks complicated, but really isn't – the black kite shape at bottom is the runway. Of importance to us are the two NDB beacons 'BN' and 'MN' and the ILS (showing 158°) (courtesy accident appendix)

The approach for Oscar Papa involved leaving the Hericourt NDB 'HR' and approaching NDB 'BN' from the west. By Hericourt, the aircraft was back on track again, having deviated previously by 5

NMs. During the approach to the Basle TMA (Terminal Management Area) the weather would have been passed by ATC to the crew.

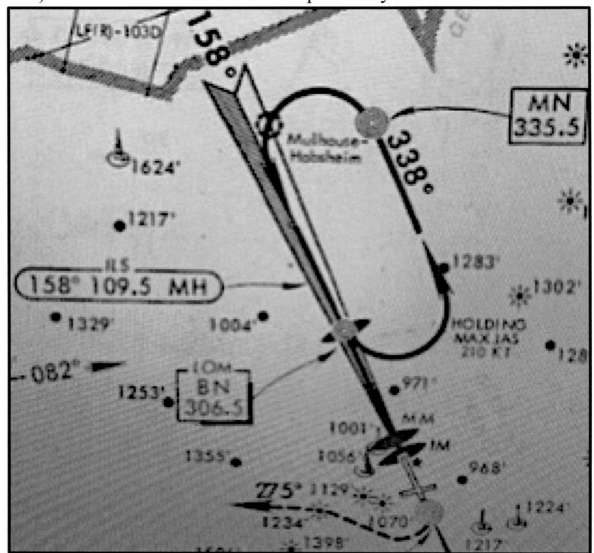

Another approach plate showing the ILS frequency (109.5 MHz) and heading (158°); note overshoot procedure at bottom (dashed line) is a sharp right turn to avoid mountains to the south (courtesy accident report appendix)

The weather passed to the crew at 08:49 local time from ATC was as follows: wind 360°/9kts, visibility (based on runway visual range equipment (RVR) A&B) A=700m, B=1300m, snow, 8/8 cloud at 120m (8/8=full cloud cover), temperature and dew point 0°C. This was a chilly spring morning, with snow, to greet the happy shoppers preparing to land. The wind was northerly but light, hence the decision by ATC to use runway 16, the instrument runway, for landings.

As the aircraft approached BN beacon, the crew called ATC, which was also equipped with VDF (VHF Direction Finder) that gives the controller a bearing to the aircraft whenever the aircraft transmits a message – there was also SRE (Secondary Surveillance Radar) at the tower, but this did not have video mapping at the time, and was thus not used for radar vectoring. There was a large cone blind spot, due to the location of the radar antenna, between BN beacon and BS beacon south of the runway (about 6 NMs in diameter). Despite this, and the handicap of snow, the approach and landing of Oscar Papa should have been fairly straight forward.

2

Just a simple approach

Calling ATC on arrival, 435 (Oscar Papa) was cleared down to 2500 feet on a local QNH setting of 998.5 millibars, and told to report at MN beacon. The time was now 08:55.48 local; from BN, the aircraft should turn left onto 338° until it reaches MN, which was transmitting on frequency 335.5 kHz (set on one of the two ADF sets). The crew would have by now also dialled up the ILS frequency of 109.5 MHz, and set the ILS heading of 158°.

The aircraft banked left, nowhere near 338° for MN beacon, but more like 290°, crossing the runway centre line about 3 NMs south-west from MN. Just before crossing the centre line, at 08:56.58, the crew of 435 radioed that they were approaching 2500 feet. The controller reminded them to 'check MN,' since they had not done so. At 08:57.42 the aircraft had crossed the runway centre line and reported '435, MN.'

The Vanguard was, at this point, still over 3 NMs short of MN, but still called ATC, who replied 'cleared for approach, check BN on final.' The aircraft should now turn left towards BN, at the same time utilizing the ILS localizer (LOC) to find the runway centre line. The glideslope (GS) would be approached from below, as is customary, and the crew then guided on a 2.5° descent to the runway threshold.

Oscar Papa turned south for about one minute, west of the runway centreline by about 2.5 NMs, then passed just north and east of BN beacon. By now, the LOC should have activated, telling the crew to steer left or right towards the runway centreline. Since there was no CVR we cannot tell what was said in the cockpit. Only the air traffic tapes give any clue. At 09:00.13 the crew radioed '435 is BN turning outbound again, will call MN.'

This is standard when a pilot messes up the approach for whatever reason. Just go around again, from BN to MN then back to BN, using LOC for lateral guidance and eventually intercepting and descending the GS. But something happened during that turn outbound from BN. The aircraft passed BN on a heading of about 120° for one mile, before banking left onto the reciprocal (300°) and passing west of BN once again, heading south-west then south, for a distance of about a mile west of the runway centreline. It then crossed the runway centreline just north of the threshold, invisible in the cloud and with ATC completely unaware of its location.

Oscar Papa was now east of the airfield, heading approximately 158° and parallel to the runway, as if making an ILS approach – it had been cleared by ATC, remember, to approach via BN. But it could not have been making a true ILS approach, since it could not pick up the GS from its location. At 09:03.38 the aircraft reported 'BN inbound,' to which air traffic replied '435, you are cleared to land on runway 16, the wind 320 degrees 8 knots.'

The Vanguard was just off the southern end of the runway at the time it reported BN inbound – but it couldn't be, for that beacon was about 5.5 NMs behind it! For the next 1½ minutes, 435 continued on a heading close to 158°, as if it was following a localizer beam about a mile east, but not on, the runway centreline. At 09:05.12 the aircraft reported overshooting. The tower seemed unconcerned, but radioed back 'okay, what do you intend to do?' Captain Anthony Dorman now took over the radio communications, indicating a change of pilot flying for the second landing attempt. He replied 'we'll try another approach.' Neither pilot wanted to upset their passengers by diverting due to bad weather.

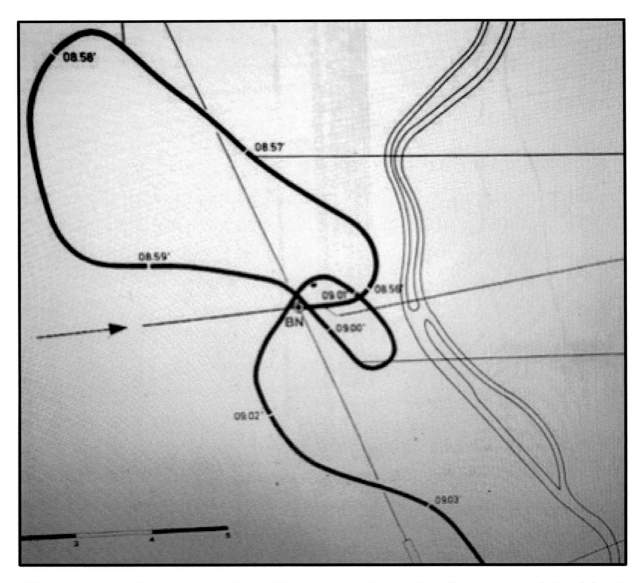

First part of the approach – 435 comes from the direction of the black arrow centre left. See text for radio transmissions with ATC (courtesy the accident report appendix)

The aircraft banked right, as per the prescribed overshoot procedure, crossed the runway centreline about 5 NMs south of the runway and returned, crossing again just south of BS beacon! The Vanguard then banked left, first reporting '435, MN,' then crossing about half the way along the active runway. The nearest beacon was the close BS beacon, transmitting on a frequency of 276.0 kHz just off the end of runway 34. The crew had two ADF sets on board, and would have selected BN (frequency 306.5 kHz) and MN (frequency 335.5 kHz) on those. The tower told 435 to report BN on finals at 09:08.51.

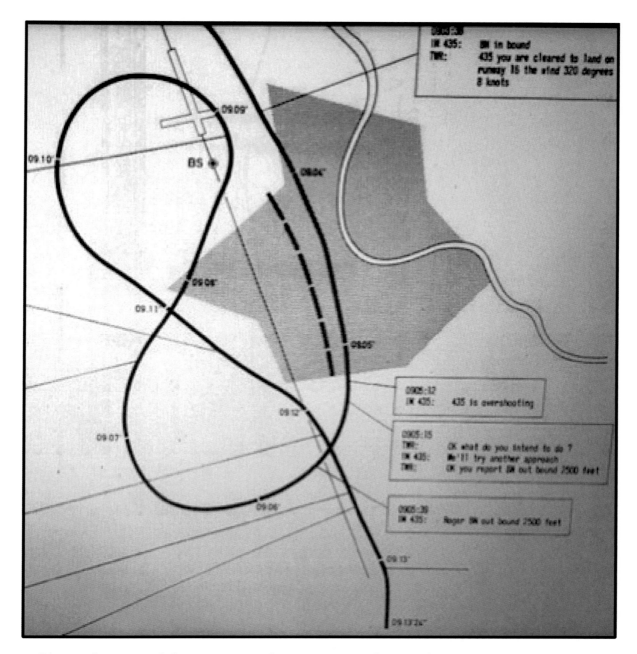

Second part of the approach – see text for radio transmissions and explanations (courtesy the accident report appendix)

ATC was not dealing with a lot of aircraft at this time, and was diverting French speaking aircraft to alternative airports because of the snow! But not 435, who would be paying higher landing fees being a foreign aircraft. At 09:11.25 Captain Dorman radioed simply 'BN.' ATC replied '435 you are cleared to land, you report light in sight, the wind now 320° 8 knots.' The controller must have been referring to the airport landing lights.

At 09:12 the aircraft crossed the runway centreline close to the ideal LOC heading of 158°. ATC suddenly took notice of the possible predicament 435 was encountering, for at 09:12.10 they radioed 'are you sure you are over BN?' To which Dorman replied 'I think've got a spurious indication. We are on the lo…on the ILS now, sir.' The tower controller replied 'Ah!'

At 09:12.33 Dorman radioed 'BN is established, on localizer and glide path, the ADF's all over the place in this weather.' The control tower finally woke up with 'for information I don't see you on my scope radar, I don't see you on my scope radar.' At 09:13.03 the tower radioed '435, what is your altitude now?' The Vanguard replied 'one thousand four hundred on the QNH.' It was the last transmission from 435. The controller replied 'Ho, I think you are on the south of the field, you are not on the…you are on the south of the field,' but nothing further was heard. At 09:13.24, Oscar Papa brushed tree tops and crashed into a mountain side, killing 108 people.

3

Investigation under way

At 09:13.40 ATC began repeatedly calling Invicta 435. At 09:20 ATC ceased calling and alerted the emergency services. At 09:30 the search and rescue service of the Federal Aviation Office and Federal Aircraft Accidents Investigation Bureau were informed that a British aircraft was thought to have crashed south of the airport. But it was not until 11:30 that the exact location of the crash was found near Hochwald, Switzerland.

Search and rescue proved difficult because of the inaccessible terrain, poor snowy weather and bad communications. But by 12:15 approximately, all those passengers rescued were under medical care; by 12:45 the most seriously injured were in hospital. The head of investigations was announced almost immediately; head of the Swiss FAAIB, K Lier. He was assisted from the UK came from J S Owen and from France, L Gueritot.

Amongst the dead were both pilots Dorman and Terry, along with two cabin attendants, Manning and Sadler – 104 passengers died, mostly women, who left 40 children back home motherless. Incredibly, 37 people survived, including cabin attendants Low (uninjured) and Axten (injured).

On the evening of the accident a British delegation arrived to assist the Swiss; amongst 12 assistants to head representative Owen were two pathologists, one odontologist, and representatives of the manufacturer, the engines and the airline. Test flights were made in the area to check that the navigation aids were operating correctly (which they were), the FDR was recovered and readings taken, and air traffic tapes listened to and transcribed.

Despite this aura of co-operation, the air traffic controllers were examined closely but not permitted to attend the public inquiry; only the director of the airport was allowed by France to attend (M A Roques). Nevertheless, it took 15 days, because of the narrow tracks, to dismantle and remove all the wreckage of the aircraft and store it at Othmarsingen, Switzerland. On day two of the rescue, two further dead bodies were recovered – apart from these people, the dead were all recovered on the afternoon of the crash.

The preliminary report into the crash was complete by 31st May 1974. The public inquiry was conducted on the 7-8th November 1974 at Solothurn, where 11 witnesses and 2 experts were examined. The readings from the MIDAS CMM/3RB FDR took some time to produce, due to errors that had to be eliminated. It is not a perfect copy of the aircraft's track to destruction, since several eye witnesses saw the Vanguard heading south in a snow storm, and their locations do not quite match that of the FDR readings.

The white oblong marks the crash site – white line is the approach and clipping of tree tops. The buildings that survivors were led to until help arrived are in the centre (courtesy Google Earth)

Most of the aircraft ended up inverted, including the centre section with part of the left wing and most of the right wing attached – the tail section was broken away and also inverted. Parts of the engines and the forward fuselage section lay scattered in an area estimated to be about 1000 square meters, facing the direction of approach.

The bodies of the two pilots underwent autopsies and nothing abnormal was found. Death was due to traumatic injuries sustained during the crash. Both men appeared to have been smokers because of high CO-Hb concentrations in their blood. Samples from the left hand control column were attributed to Captain Dorman, who must therefore have been seated in that seat.

There was very little fire after the accident, and that around the right wing was extinguished by the first people on the site. Those who survived the crash appeared to have been sitting in the rear section of the Vanguard when it clipped trees and somersaulted into the Swiss mountain. With regard to the FDR, it only recorded 6 parameters: indicated air speed (IAS), altitude; vertical acceleration; magnetic heading, pitch attitude and time signals.

The only equipment available to transcribe this FDR was in Bournemouth, UK, so it was here that it was transcribed and refined with the help of a computer. The final flight path had only a narrow margin of error. With regards to wind direction and speed, only an average could be obtained, leading to a lateral deviation of about 800m compared to eye witness reports (see second part of the approach on page 15 – the broken line indicates where eye witnesses say they saw Oscar Papa, which differs from the FDR). Things get a little technical now, for a while – so try and remember any physics lessons!

On the 21st November 1973 a test aircraft calibrated the ground aids to navigation at Basle, and particularly the ILS. No defects were found in the equipment; a number of LOC back beams, and GS secondary beams, were identified as expected, and these we shall look at later. Examination by investigators of the flap actuating cylinder in the right wing and the flap selector box recovered from the wreckage, showed that the landing flaps were extended to the 20° position at impact. Elevator trim was at 1.0 nose up position, with the directional trim at 0.5 divisions left and aileron trim neutral.

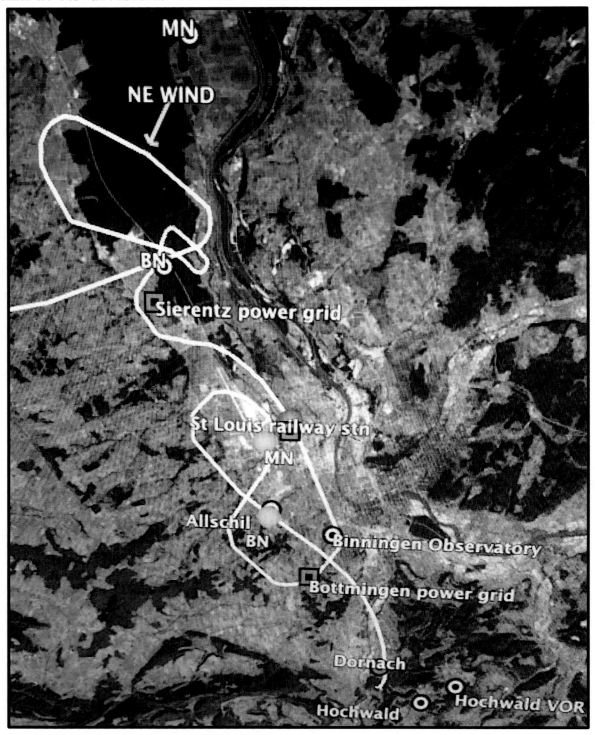

The route as per the FDR – the Vanguard never reached the real MN NDB, and called BN three times and MN twice; the yellow dots were spurious calls from the cockpit. Why? (courtesy Google Earth)

The four engine compressors and propellers were under power at the time of the crash, although investigators could not determine what power setting was used. It is important to know what was tuned to which equipment in the cockpit, so these are listed here:

VHF/COMS 1 – 126.80 MHz (Geneva Met broadcast)

VHF/COMS 2 – 118.30 MHz (Basle tower).

VHF/NAV 1 & 2 – both tuned to 109.5 MHz (Basle ILS)

VOR – Unit 1 – inexpert repairs had been carried out but did not affect performance. The VOR flag alarm was set at a slightly too high flag current. The LOC alarm circuit was set far above nominal values; the warning flag did not appear even when unusable signals were received. Deflection sensitivity was set 50% too high.

VOR – Unit 2 – a modification from service information letter 12-63 of 6th June 1963 had not been implemented. Its non-implementation did not affect the performance of the VOR 2 unit in the aircraft, however.

Glideslope Receiver 1 – No irregularities found.

Glideslope Receiver 2 – Alarm circuit was set too high; the warning flag did not appear even when unusable signals were received.

Marker Receiver – was live at the time of crash.

ADF 1 – possible intermittent electrical interruptions in loop servo amplifier were caused by poorly soldered joints. At the time of the crash it was tuned to 335 kHz (335.5 kHz is the MN NDB). Inexpertly carried out repairs were found in the loop servo amplifier.

ADF 2 – at the time of the crash this was working and tuned to 306 kHz (BN NDB is 306.5 kHz). It is interesting to note that neither ADF was fully tuned – the decimal point part was missing, but it is possible this is because of the type of ADF installed.

Autopilot - Heading mode was selected for the Integrated Flight System (IFS) but investigators could not determine whether the autopilot was engaged.

De-icing equipment – the wing leading edge de-icing equipment was not switched on at the time of the crash.

Altimeter 1: set to 967mb (the QFE at the time – it should have been 967.5mb – this is airfield level).

Altimeter 2: set to 997mb (the QNH at the time – the correct QNH was 998.5mb – the difference in millibars was 1.5mb, or 45 feet in altitude).

RMI (Radio Magnetic Indicator)/VOR/ADF compass: jammed at 200°, corresponding with the aircraft's course at the time of the crash.

Course indicators: both were jammed at 158°, corresponding with the ILS LOC course (QFU) for runway 16.

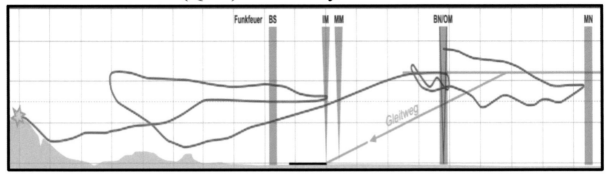

From the FDR the vertical profile of 435; this includes the two descents to overshoot (red). Also the aircraft had decided to overshoot a second time and was climbing when it hit trees (far left). Purple vertical lines are navigation beacons, right to left: MN, BN/OM, MM, IM, BS

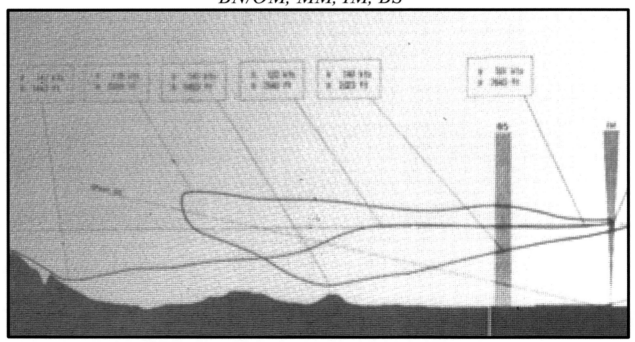

Above: speed profile boxes (from right to left)

Box top right (next to inner marker IM): V (velocity) 161 kts, H (height) 2643 feet.

Next box (left, next to BS NDB second approach): V 148 kts H 2023 feet

Next box (left, final approach): V 133 kts H 2643 feet

Next box (left, overshoot second approach): V 141 kts, H 1403 feet

Next box (left, overshoot climb, second approach): V 178 kts, H 3333 feet

Final box (far left, final overshoot): V 147 kts H 1443 feet

4

Grand discoveries

Most of the information so far has come as a result the accident investigations between the Swiss, French and British. The British team did quite a thorough investigation into G-AXOP's history. Only the day before the fatal crash, the aircraft was positioned at Luton airport, ready to fly to Bristol to collect the passengers. On final approach using ILS, the co-pilot saw a discrepancy between the instrument indications of the pilot-in-command and the co-pilot.

The co-pilot's ADF and localizer needle showed a definite deviation to the left of the approach path, whilst the pilot-in-command's instruments showed the aircraft on the centreline. Shortly after reporting this, the crew became visual with the ground and Oscar Papa was indeed flying left of the centreline. No entry was made in the technical log because on landing, the readings on the integrated flight system (IFS) and ILS instruments all read the same.

The incident was reported to the duty engineer at Luton, who could not recall any such conversation. The co-pilot did inform the crew flying to Bristol, so both Captains Dorman and Terry must have known. It was reported to the superiors of the first crew, who noted the discrepancy, but it was not until six months later, after the fatal crash, that investigators got to know of it.

IFS (Integrated Flight System): this supplies computed control signals for the bank required to maintain a desired course; it is displayed on the left/right artificial horizons. It operates in three modes: Heading, Nav/Loc and Approach.

Heading: the steering pointer position depends on the difference between the heading selected and that flown, instantaneous bank and yaw rate. The steering pointer shows zero when the actual heading and the selected heading are identical, with zero bank/yaw.

Nav/Loc: this is used for VOR or ILS. It operates similarly to Heading mode, the selected course being here a VOR radial or the ILS heading against the actual heading, deviation from the beam (VOR or ILS), instantaneous bank and yaw rates. Any deviation from the nominal flight path immediately gives rise to the appropriate control signal.

Approach: this is selected when the aircraft is established on the localizer, and the glideslope pointer has reached zero. Any deviation from the nominal flight path immediately gives rise to the appropriate control signal.

That's most of the technical stuff out of the way, from which you might deduce the complexity of flying; likewise, the assistance available in the cockpit to help the pilot. One of those devices is the ADF, which works in conjunction with ground based NDB beacons. We've seen that there was confusion of sorts on the flight deck, with the crew radioing BN three times, only one of which was actually over the beacon and the other two spurious and unexplained; the first spurious, during Dorman's first approach, was called in about 6 NMs south of the actual beacon – the second spurious, during Terry's second approach, was called in just over 8 NMs south of the actual beacon.

How was this possible? Perhaps there was an intermittent fault in the system? The history of the two ADF systems on Oscar Papa were examined closely during investigations. Between May and June 1972, Invicta crews complained about ADF 1, but according to Invicta records, ADF 2 was replaced with a repaired unit, rather than a new, more expensive ADF. In July 1972 a complaint was made about ADF 1; no fault was found but the system so 1 and 2 were interchanged.

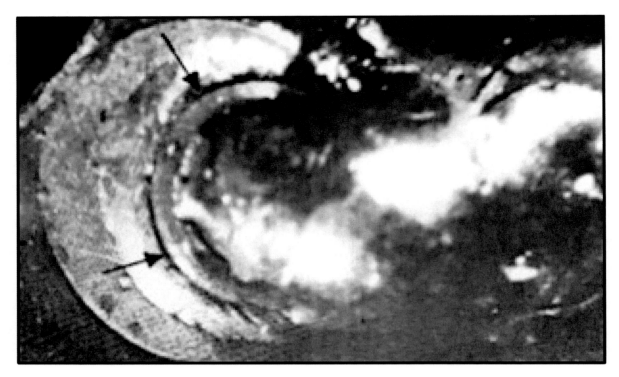

From the accident report – example of 'bad' soldering in the ADF 1 loop servo amplifier (courtesy UK accident report)

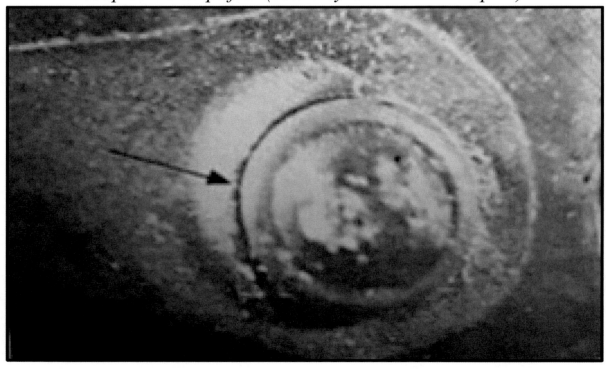

From the accident report – further example of 'bad' soldering in the ADF 1 loop servo amplifier (courtesy UK accident report)

Work on the aircraft was carried out for Invicta by Aviation Traders (Engineering) Ltd, or ATEL. The airline was not licenced to carry out repairs on any radio equipment independently, so this work was carried out under the supervision of ATEL technicians. Most of the work was carried out at Manston, Kent, or occasionally Luton.

The aircraft's technical logs do not indicate just when the VOR 1 / Glide Slope 2 receivers were incorrectly set, nor when the botched soldering work was done. The Swiss would be quick in attributing many of these faults as causes to the crash – in all likelihood, they did not help matters, yet the equipment continued to function satisfactorily most of the time.

Let's turn next to the weather – was it below minimums at the time, and should ATC have sent Oscar Papa away? The Vickers Vanguard was considered, for instrument approaches, a Cat.II type aircraft – a precision approach to a lower minimum was not possible, because the aircraft lacked a 'radar' altimeter. But for Oscar Papa's purposes, a standard ILS approach had the following minimum: minimum height 65m (213 feet) and a minimum visibility of 600m (1968 feet).

It is the airlines responsibility, as you would expect, to make sure its pilots observe the minimums for any airport, and also the crews to work within company minimums and their own level of competency. Much depends on the ILS/radar/approach lighting/runway length of an airport – for Basle, the minimums in the Invicta flight operations manual were 250 feet / 650m (2132 feet). The Jeppesen manual carried on the aircraft had minimums of 200 feet / 750m (2460 feet). The instrument approach to Basle is considered operationally simple to achieve.

The weather passed by ATC to the crew at 08:49 was visibility between 700m and 1300m along the runway, and cloud base (8/8[ths]) of 120m (393 feet) – all within the airport minimums and within the flight operations manual. So, the weather, from an ATC point of view, was above minimums. The type of weather, however, was snow. Therefore, the landing aids, the NDB's, should, according to ICAO regulations, operate on an AO/A2 type of emission.

Yet the two main approach aids, beacons BN and MN, were operating on a AO/A1 type of emission – with unmodulated carrier, which causes the ADF needle to oscillate during keying of station identification. The French operating authorities justify this inferior type of beacon because of the narrower band width, allowing more beacons within a band wave.

Air traffic control are the people responsible for seeing the safe and expeditious arrival and departure of aircraft. There were two types of ATC affecting Oscar Papa – approach control, and aerodrome control (the tower). When traffic was light, aerodrome control was permitted to operate both approach and aerodrome control. When traffic was heavy, the two services operated separately.

Control of the aircraft was to be handed from approach to aerodrome control when the approaching aircraft had the runway insight. When Oscar Papa contacted Basle, it was handed over right away to aerodrome control, where the controller was fully qualified to operate approach. However, this handover was contrary to the rules just mentioned, since Oscar Papa did not have the runway in sight.

The aerodrome controller in the tower has the same radar set available as the approach controller did, who likely sat in a darkened room inside the same control tower. The radar scope is called a PPI, or Plan Position Indicator, and provides the following services to the controller: radar information and radar surveillance. Oscar Papa was handed over to the aerodrome controller for the approach on frequency 118.3 MHz, without the runway being in sight as should have been the case.

By doing this, the use of the Basle VDF, a VHF direction finder that points towards the radio transmission from a pilot, was lost to the tower controller. According to the accident report, notification of the runway visual range (RVR) was given on first contact with Oscar Papa by ATC; however, a deteriorating RVR below airport minimums (700m) was not passed on – the fact that visibility was poor in the area was passed on, in French, to another aircraft.

5

What the Swiss said (bullet points)

(My comments, where necessary, are in brackets and italics. This is an abridged version):

° The flight crew was qualified, medically fit and rested prior to the accident, according to the Swiss accident report.

° Disturbances due to static are customary for NDBs operating in areas of active snowfall.

° From 09:03 to 09:09, the RVR at Basle airport fell below the minimums of 700m – to between 500m and 550m, well below that for a Vanguard aircraft. This was not notified to the crew. At the time the aircraft was just overshooting from its first attempt to land, and was heading north to try and find MN and BN.

° Any changes in weather has to come from a qualified meteorologist (*in France*), and the controller felt not obliged to report the dip in RVR until the Met people had officially contacted him; also, things had improved over the airfield, although not on the approach to runway 16. However, this did not stop him reporting the facts, in French, to another aircraft.

° In the crash area, the cloud was continuous and visibility so poor that, combined with the snow covered ground and lack of contrast, the crew could not see the ground in time to avoid it. The aircraft was not equipped with a ground proximity warning system (GPWS) (*nor radar altimeter*).

° Despite the poor weather, the ADF/NDB signals were still usable. During the critical times of 04:00 and 10:30, ten aircraft landed safely at Basle and two aircraft diverted to different airfields.

° The ADF/NDB signals were usable on the aircraft at least much of the time during the flight and approach; Hericourt (HR) beacon was passed normally, and on the approach from HR to BN, the track was constant with BN passed over correctly twice. During the second attempt to land, it is possible the crew mistook the NDB BS beacon for the MN beacon (*the frequency for BS was 276 kHz and MN was 335.5 kHz – unless the wrong frequency was entered, it is not possible for BS to be indicating if MN was selected – more about later*).

° Monitoring the ILS and markers would be possible using VOR/DME with no electrostatic interference; VDF (radial) could have been requested from ATC, but was not (*had approach control not been handed over early to aerodrome control on frequency 118.3 MHz then the controller at any time could have checked upon the aircraft's progress*).

° ATC were aware of the shortcomings of medium wave beacons in the Basle TMA, and lengthy endeavours were in place to acquire an electrostatic free VOR beacon (*there wasn't one at Basle at the time of the accident, although the Vanguard was equipped to use VOR had one been in place. Since France maintained the ATC system, it was down to France to pay for a VOR – this they had not done at the time of the accident*).

° The repetition of the procedure turns over BN should have been given more alertness by ATC – this manoeuvre rarely happens, and is usually caused by navigational inaccuracies or technical defects on board the aircraft.

° A former captain's report to ATC by telephone of a low flying aircraft over Binnigen should have had a disquieting effect, as should have the reported overshoot in view of the weather conditions over the airfield at the time – something the air traffic controller had not considered critical (*see next chapter on the Binnigen observatory incident*).

° A call from Zurich Area Control Centre (*about an aircraft heading south*) was very alarming and confirmed by the air traffic controller's own radar scope, but did not prompt the controller to take immediate and determined action – although no other aircraft could have been operating in that area because of the weather. The controller did not intervene with specific information until it was too late (*see next chapter on the Zurich ACC incident*).

° It must be remembered that radar and VDF could have helped detect incorrect flight paths and for ATC to take early action to help the cockpit crew.

° Air traffic services (ATS) were not designed to give warning when an aircraft infringed the required minimum height above ground level.

° ATC cannot undertake warning aircraft for infringing the required minimum height above ground level if, like at Basle, no precision approach radar (PAR) is available.

° The whole ATC system has an unwritten inherent duty to draw the attention of other users of the system to obviously dangerous situations even though the duty to warn is not part of their primary duty. Greater attentiveness and active helpfulness would have been expected.

° The dubious basic training of Captain Dorman and inconsistences in his flying log book cannot be blamed upon the airline; they could also have found out from the British licencing authority the difficulty it took for him to obtain the British instrument rating (*it took him 9 attempts to obtain it – he was Canadian by birth and had trained in the Canadian armed forces as a pilot, which was soon discontinued due to his lack of aptitude. He later obtained the relevant licences abroad. Until the crash, he had flown two instrument approaches to Basle with Captain Terry*).

° Flight path interpretation: the unreported deviation from the airway centreline between Rolampont and Hericourt could have been caused by more favourable conditions for descent south of the airway (*or also, faulty ADF equipment on the aircraft, or strong north blowing winds*). The high airspeed established at the same time might be explained by a descent in a cloud gap (*here the report begins a series of surmises*).

° Preparation for first approach attempt: the first procedure turn is characterized by inaccurate course selection at the wrong interception angle and therefore did not lead to the prescribed MN beacon – but probably unnoticed at the time, crossed the localizer beam. When roughly abeam MN the aircraft reported passing it.

The first procedural turn at BN – the aircraft should have headed 338° to MN but didn't, missing the beacon by over 3 NMs (courtesy accident report appendix)

A consistent intercept course was maintained to BN, during which maintenance of height was poor, fluctuating between 2200 feet and 2900 feet – the assigned altitude was 2500 feet. Turbulence alone cannot explain this deviation, as acceleration recorded on the FDR was only slight. As this procedure turn took them beyond the ILS localizer path, a second attempt was inevitable, during which the crew must have made a crucial navigation error – quite obviously confusing beacons MN and BN. In an extremely tight turn, during which the aircraft deviated from the assigned height by 950 feet, they headed straight for BN and passed it at a height of 3200 feet, where the assigned height was 1923 feet (*there is no explanation, if turbulence was not to blame, for the variations in height – only that the FDR must have been inaccurate, or the readings misread. As for confusing the navaids, even if it were so the compass needles for both MN and BN would have been pointing behind the aircraft, since both beacons were behind it. More explanation in next chapter*).

° First approach attempt: after passing BN the aircraft descended with a remarkably constant rate of descent, at first considerably to the right and later to the left of the ILS centreline. When abeam the BS beacon, the aircraft reported BN, suggesting these beacons were confused. The aircraft descended to 1400 feet before overshooting over Basle city, where it was seen by several witnesses. It is to be assumed that the crew, like several of the surviving passengers, could see the ground, above all through the side windows, and therefore initiated the overshoot after some hesitation before reaching the ILS minimum of 1133 feet (*again, more assumptions; aircrew on instruments in poor weather would be looking ahead for the runway lights, not glancing out of the side windows. None of the navigation equipment recovered from the wreckage showed any navaid tuned to 276 kHz, the frequency for BS beacon at the south end of the runway. This first approach was conducted by Captain Dorman in the left hand seat, because his blood was found on the control column and Captain Terry was identified as the pilot using the radio until the overshoot*).

° Second attempt approach: coincident with this first overshoot is a change of operator of the radio, implying a change of pilot flying (*Terry flying instead of Dorman*). Afterwards, the flight path is much smoother regards course and height. The flight proceeded in a wide turn to the right, towards the BS beacon and a height of 3200 feet, which was slowly reduced to the assigned level of 2500 feet for a long time. In the vicinity of BS beacon, MN was reported and left hand turn initiated to the west of the localizer which was approached in a clean (as such wrong) intercept. The localizer back beam once reached was maintained accurately and the second approach initiated. The aircraft reached a point where the glide path warning flag had to be visible the whole time, at least on the captain's instrument, because the glide path signal was too weak in that area. At 1400 feet an abrupt overshoot was initiated, which was felt by the surviving passengers. The aircraft climbed at optimum rate, before the high rate of climb was soon decreased somewhat with the result that the aircraft hit the upper slopes of the range of hills and was wrecked (*more about ILS back beams in the next chapter*).

° Swiss Air Accident Report Summary: the flight path during descent from HR to BN was normal, then becomes highly erratic with regards to navigation and maintenance of height, deviating considerably from the prescribed flight path and height. During the second procedure turn before final approach, a navigational error was obviously made, as the aircraft headed for BN again instead of MN. One cannot say whether this was due to the fact that the two beacons were not set on the ADFs in the normal sequence (ADF 1 – BN, ADF 2 – MN). The opposite settings were found in the wreckage.

Following the second procedure turn a continual descent begins from a height of 3200 feet, as if they had a definite glade path indication. This could not, however, have come from the ILS transmitter, as the flight path led over the glide path station with its many weak and steep secondary glide path beams.

At approximately 3200 feet over BN a spurious glide path was crossed during the second procedure turn. If on the basis of this, and with a localizer indication, the flight director (FD) was set to approach mode in order to follow both pointers (*that is, the LOC pointer and the GS pointer*) on this, the subsequent approach might be explained, but only if the two pilots neglected to keep the normal, continuous and mutual check on the basic navigation instruments and the marker control (*inner marker IM, middle marker MM, outer marker OM*).

The reason for the poor ILS tracking during the first attempt can be explained by the defect found in the captain's ILS equipment. It is extremely disturbing that the deflection sensitivity of the localizer had been set 50% too high. Because of this, the localizer indication and therefore the IFS steering pointer were so jittery that they could hardly be followed anymore.

It was also easy to miss crossing the localizer on the second procedure turn, as this lasted only 3 or 4 seconds instead of the usual 10. The unrectified, temporary defect in the captain's ILS equipment of the previous day, where the aircraft flew left of the centre line, indicates that it may have recurred, certainly for the first approach attempt. The markers were not used to identify the beacons and the correct glide path altitude (*the markers could not be used as the aircraft was nowhere near them for most of the time*).

The crew's conduct following discontinuation of the first approach attempt is inexplicable. Although it must be assumed on the basis of the witness statements and the plot of the flight path that the crew realized what a dangerous manoeuvre they had carried out – instead of the un-built up and flat outlying ground of the aerodrome a densely populated and hilly area came into view even before the normal ILS approach minimum was reached – no fundamentally new safety measures were taken.

In view of the 'bungled' situation the crew did not request ATC assistance, nor did they attempt the second approach using only localizer, glide path and time/course navigation. The second approach attempt being initiated with the position report MN in the vicinity of BS shows further confusion of navigational aids.

Findings

The licences of the crew were in order and valid. They were authorized to operate the flight and had landed at Basle several times before.

There were no reasons to believe the crew had any medical disorders during the flight.

The aircraft was declared airworthy and was certified.

There were no signs of structural failure, fire on board, engine or control failure.

There were several faults in the radio-navigation equipment, making the crew's navigational orientation more difficult.

In the prevailing meteorological conditions atmospheric disturbances impaired the reception of the medium wave navigational beacons. They still gave usable indications as least part of the time.

According to the data record of automatic equipment, the visibility conditions on the instrument runway was at times below the minimum for the aircraft type. They were not communicated to the crew.

The first procedural turn over BN had to be repeated because of navigational difficulties that arose.

The first approach resulted in a near accident far from the aerodrome after the crew established visual contact with the ground.

The second approach was initiated south of Basle airport without using the ILS marker beacons.

The overshoot during the second unsuccessful approach was initiated too late so that G-AXOP, while still airworthy, crashed into steep wooded terrain.

Probable causes of the accident

The accident was attributable to:

° loss of orientation during two ILS approaches carried out under instrument flight conditions.

The following contributed to the accident

° inadequate navigation, above all imprecise initiation of final approach as regards height and approach axis.

° confusion of navigational aids.

° insufficient checking and comparison of navigational aids and instrument readings (cross and double checks).

° the poor reception of the medium wave beacons, the technical defects in LOC receiver and glideslope receiver no.2 made the crews task more difficult.

Recommendations

° radar vectoring should be provided at Basle.

° medium wave beacons adjusted to a modulation in conformity with ICAO.

° suppression of unpublicized ILS back beams, especially glide path back beams.

° official approach charts should contain indications for cross checking the main approach beacon with other electrostatic-free radio aids.

° all commercial aircraft with an all-up weight more than 5700 kgs should be equipped with flight data and cockpit voice recorders.

° all commercial aircraft with an all-up weight more than 5700 kgs should be equipped with a ground proximity warning device.

The gymnasium at Dornach and the coffins of the dead

6

ATC incidents and other things

Phew! That was the gist of what happened to the 108 dead people on board G-AXOP. Their pilots became disorientated, failed to cross check their navigation instruments, confused their navigation beacons, and attempted two ILS landings without appearing to know exactly where they were, in deteriorating weather conditions, with faulty equipment on board and without asking for ATC assistance.

You might have detected a note of cynicism in the Swiss report towards the French air traffic controllers, and also the French authorities responsible for operating and maintaining the navigation equipment. Rather than spend money, the French allowed vital equipment to remain of inferior standard; the NDB beacons at Basle were of the older AOA1 type, rather than the more reliable AOA2.

Negotiations had been on going to install an electrostatic free VOR navaid at Basle. ATC would have benefitted from the use of precision approach radar (PAR) rather than the simpler precision plan position indicator (PPI) type installed at Basle. Nevertheless, ATC there committed a number of other things that did not help Oscar Papa.

The deterioration in RVR to 500 – 550 meters was not reported to the crew, although controllers sought to advise French speaking aircraft approaching to divert. Apparently, they had to wait for qualified meteorologists to confirm the weather, before it could be broadcast to aircraft.

The transfer of approach control work to aerodrome control meant the VDF service was not working, although there was no reason for the aircraft to request the service on another radio channel. This would have meant the approach controller going back to their radar scope and operating some equipment.

The Binningen incident

This involved directly Basle ATC and a former airline captain who happened to be at Binningen observatory. This was Mr R Beck, who put through a call to Basle tower at 09:08.10 that morning, about three minutes after 435 reported it was overshooting for the first time. Here is the transcript:

TWR – Basle ATC tower, BECK – R Beck (at Binningen)

TWR – hello

BECK – hello the tower

TWR – yes good morning

BECK – yes good morning monsieur, this is Beck at the Basle – Binningen observatory

TWR – yes

BECK – there is an aircraft which has just passed two minutes ago heading south

TWR – yes

BECK – ah, probably aha four-engined turbo-prop

TWR – yes

BECK – probably, and it is flying at barely 50 metres and then it is snowing very heavily and I have the impression if it remains like this it will crash in the mountains

TWR – ah hold on you are really sure that is flying at 50 metres?

BECK – yes certainly listen, I was a pilot with Swissair I have just now retired ba

TWR – ah, agreed (two conversations simultaneously)

BECK – I work here (two conversations simultaneously) …I am telephoning you it was here at a maximum of 50 metres south of the observatory here

An aside from M Mao can be heard now 'an aircraft which was flying at 50 metres above the observatory, everything was blotted out, it is a former Swissair pilot who is on the telephone.'

TWR – right, thank you

BECK – it had a red tail unit, I could not I did not have time to see the markings

TWR – yes but because you are being…(pause)…there is an aircraft which has just overshot there which is going to return over…... (two conversations simultaneously)

BECK – it must be made to climb

TWR – yes agreed thank you

BECK – it must be made to climb; it is going to crash in the mountains like this

TWR – agreed thank you

BECK – well then many thanks goodbye

TWR – goodbye

BECK – goodbye

Call ends at 09:09.10, after exactly one minute. During it, the controller talks by radio to 435; the aircraft reports MN and the controller says '435 report BN on final.' The Vanguard replies 'roger.' Just how Mr R Beck must have felt when he heard the news of the fatal air crash in the mountains later that day can only be imagined.

<u>The Zurich Area Control Centre incident</u>

As if having the civilian Mr R Beck telephoning you in the tower about an aircraft flying at just 50m southbound in a snow storm, ATC at Basle also took a call from the Zurich Area Control Centre. This was about two minutes after Beck's call, at 09:11.10. A radar operator in Zurich ACC west sector, observes an unidentified echo (unknown traffic) 3-5 NMs south-west of Basle heading towards HOC.

B/M – Basle aerodrome controller, ZH – Zurich ACC

B/M – yes hello

Z/H – tell me, you have someone who has taken off who is now crawling towards Hochwald?

B/M – ah! Who is on the Hochwald side? We have an aircraft which has overshot, yes, but it is going to return to BN.

The Binningen incident – the location of the observatory close to the approximate first overshoot line (white) (courtesy Google Earth)

Binningen Observatory (bottom left, green building) and approximate flight path of G-AXOP (white line); this prompted R Beck to call the control tower and warn them of a stray aircraft (courtesy Google Earth)

Z/H – ah! It is…

B/M – hold on hold on

Z/H – it has a heading for Hochwald

B/M – what?

The Basle controller radios to 435, who has just called BN. '435 you are cleared to land you report light in sight the wind now 320/8kts' The Vanguard replied simply 'thank you.'

Z/H – it has a heading for Hochwald

B/M – towards Hochwald, hold on

Z/H – what is its flight level?

B/M – ah! Yes, I see one in that direction which is heading for Hochwald now you will be told that at once…

Basle aerodrome controller observes unidentified radar echo 6 NMs south of the aerodrome along the runway centreline.

B/M – yes hello, you must check with Paris because the aircraft has supposedly passed BN it has just contacted us ours has passed BN

Z/H – it is probably a VFR but that's not on now

B/M – eh

Z/H – we cannot see it any more now, eh right agreed many thanks

B/M – yes right

Z/H – thank you

B/M - cheers

Call ends 09:12.10

This is when the penny finally drops and the ATC controller at Basle tower suddenly sees an unidentified blip on radar. At 09:12.10, as the phone call from Zurich ends, Basle is on the radio.

TWR – 'Invicta 435 Basle.'

435 – '435.'

TWR – 'are you sure, you are over BN?'

435 – 'I think've got a spurious indication. We are on the lo…on the ILS now, sir.'

TWR – 'ah!'

435 – 'BN is established on localizer and glide path the ADFs all over the place in this weather.'

TWR – 'for information I don't see you on my scope radar I don't see you on my scope radar.'

TWR – '435 what is your altitude now?'

435 – 'one thousand four hundred on the QNH.'

TWR – 'Ho, I think you are on south of the field, you are not on the…you are on the south of the field.'

Thirty seconds later the controller was calling 435. There was no reply. Now another thing we've heard about is the ILS back beam. Normally there is a glide slope beam from the active runway, pointing out into the approach at an angle of between 2.5° and 3°. Often, unless suppressed, there is beam going in the opposite direction, too. This can often be used to line up and approach the runway from the opposite direction.

Aerial shot – wreckage (circle), tree tops hit (black arrow, right), nearest buildings (bottom left) (courtesy the accident report)

Many older systems of ILS have not only a front beam and a back beam, but other 'ghost' beams at steeper angles, which are not suppressed and usually, under normal circumstances, do not interfere with an ILS approach. But circumstances were not normal on the day that Oscar Papa crashed. Check the diagram from the Swiss accident report below.

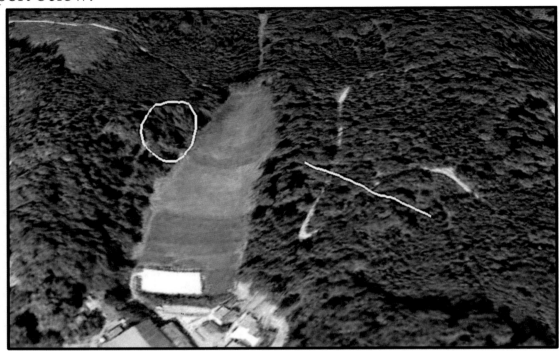

The crash site today (courtesy Google Earth)

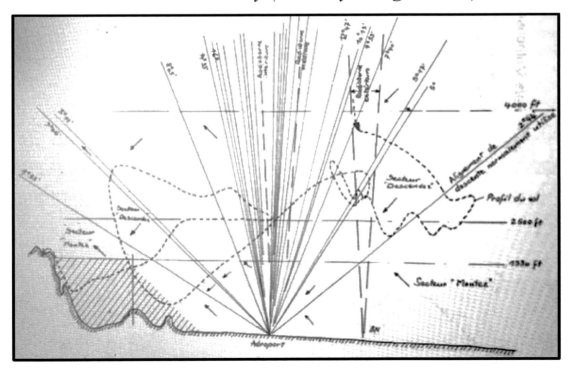

Above: unsuppressed 'ghost' glide slope beams at Basle from accident report with G-AXOP's vertical path (broken lines). Normal GS is on the right, at 2°44' (courtesy the accident appendix)

The normal GS angle for Basle is 2°44' and is on the far right of the diagram above. If you follow the two descent profiles for the aircraft above, (the broken lines), you can see that the first descent profile (Captain Dorman – centre left) runs parallel to the 2°44' beam, although about 8kms (4.9 miles) south of it.

The second profile (Captain Terry on far left) runs parallel to Dorman's but farther south, about 3kms (1.8 miles) beyond Dorman's attempt; note it becomes steeper in descent before becoming shallower prior to overshooting and crashing.

Note the 'ghost' signals from the GS transmitter, that may, under the weather conditions prevailing at the time, have interfered with the GS indications in the cockpit. From right to left they are: 5°, 5°17', 7°40', 10°15', 12°47' to the centre. From left to right to the centre they are: 1°55', 3°06', 3°11', 8°05', 14°35', and 16°.

Anyone of these could have caused the ILS equipment on Oscar Papa to give a false GS reading, and allow the aircraft to fly into the ground unless the pilots could see where they were flying – which they could not. But it's also highly likely they would be aware of a steeper angle of descent, for example 5° rather than 2.5°, due to increasing accelerations. In the final chapter, we will see that, despite the findings of the Swiss accident report and the ineptitude (until too late) of French air traffic control, Oscar Papa was actually lured to destruction by another phantom force.

7

Lured to death

In January of 1978 a new report was issued by Jean Forestier regarding the disaster that befell G-AXOP on a Swiss mountain side. It was suggested, and rightly so in my opinion, that there had been illegal radio transmissions from the French electricity company, *Electricite de France*, in certain regions around Basle on the day of the G-AXOP disaster.

Because of the weather conditions, these transmissions were broadcast along the national grid or the overhead railway power cables, on frequencies very close to those of the BN/MN medium wave navigation beacons.

I don't pretend, of course, to be an expert in this field either, so I will try to keep it all abridged and simple. How were these illegal transmissions possible, you may well ask? Such things had been happening in the UK as far back as 1966, when the Central Electricity Generating Board (CEGB) commenced not only sending electricity down the power lines of the national grid, but messages, too. The sort of things that might be sent would be power consumption figures at certain times of day, between one power generating station and another.

A useful thing to do, you might say, if you're into power generating? Sustained use of the cables, as opposed to sending just a brief message as had been the case from the 1940's, required a newer process called 'continuous carrier-frequency signalling' (CCFS). The electric current traveling through a cable makes the cable act just like a radio transmitting aerial. From the grid power lines, however, the signals should emit no farther than 200m from the source – the frequencies selected by the CEGB were the 200-500 KHz band.

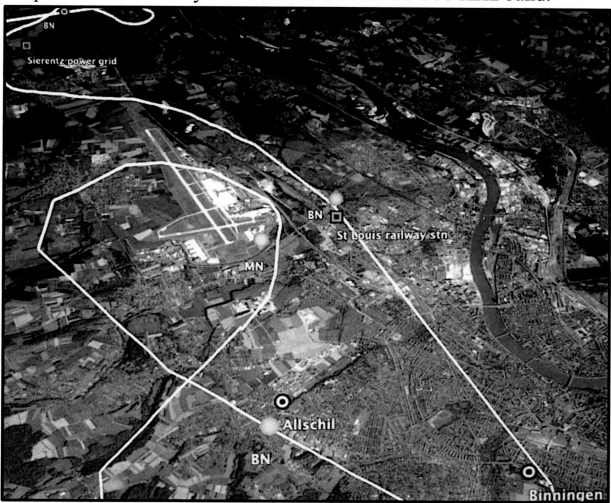

The three spurious ghost beacons (yellow) and two of three power grid/rail lines responsible (red) (courtesy Google Earth)

As you might deduce, these frequencies also included those of air traffic navigation equipment! And it was not long before aircraft stacked over Watford one night were radioing trouble with their radio compasses. Investigations revealed the holding beacons were being interfered with by signals from power lines. The CEGB stopped sending signals right away. Wet weather at the time was found to be the cause of the interference.

The full explanation was that the cable insulators caused short circuits, if exposed to heavy rain, snow, sleet, ice, mist, fog or drizzle.

During such a short circuit, the signals emitted farther than just 200m! Sensitive aircraft compasses would swing towards the short circuited power lines, the navigational beacon, or somewhere in between.

Despite various international conferences, the problem regarding these transmissions was not eradicated, and some countries, France and Switzerland amongst them, continued using their power grids for message transmission. A precursor to Basle occurred in France just six months before, on 27th October 1972.

Noiretable Air Crash

You would think this sort of accident would alert the *Electricite de France* into action, but no; perhaps it was too close to the Basle crash for an accident report to be completed? Air Inter flight 696Y was a Vickers Viscount and took off from Lyon for Clermont-Ferrand on an evening flight of about 85 miles. On board were 68 people, including children.

The weather in the area ahead was rain and low cloud. ATC wanted to put the aircraft into a hold prior to landing, and the holding should have been over the NDB CF, about 9 NMs from the Clermont-Ferrand runway threshold. Instead, the aircraft appears to have entered

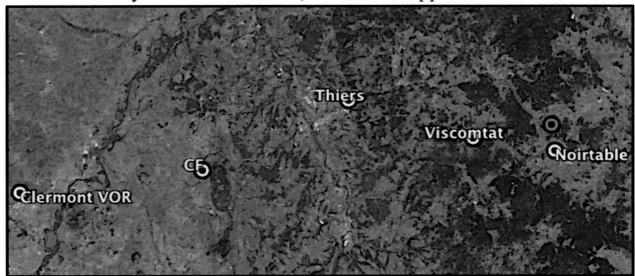

Noirtable crash – red mark is the crash site, CF is the NDB, Clermont VOR is at the airport (courtesy Google Earth)

a holding pattern more than 40kms from the airport, near Noirtable, descending on the instructions of ATC and circling at least twice before hitting high ground. Sixty people died and 8 survived, including some children. Amongst those killed was Captain Bonnell, co-pilot Aubert, training pilot Lapierre, hostess Audibert and steward David.

Like the Basle air crash and the Dan Air Tenerife disaster of 1980, there is very little information on the Noirtable accident. Even the accident report, naturally, is in French. I have tried a little translation here on just the Viscount's ATC communications, since ATC did have other aircraft under control at the time, and I believe there was confusion on the Viscount flight deck.

TWR – '696Y Clermont, your level?'

696Y – '55 in descent.'

TWR – '55 descending, received' (then clears IT537 down to 60 and to call when approaching that level).

The crash site today, with white crucifix marker in memory of those who died at Noirtable.

696Y – 'correction, 65 descending now.'

TWR – (clears IT537 now to 70, instead).

696Y – 'I've arrived at 50.'

TWR – 'you continue to 3600.'

TWR – (clears IT537 from 70 to 50 in the NDB CF stack).

696Y – 'in procedure turn.'

TWR – 'you continue, report CF on ILS.'

696Y – 'okay.'

TWR – 'wind calm.' (ATC deals further with IT537).

TWR – '696 Clermont, position?'

IT537 – '696Y, Clermont is calling you.'

TWR – '696Y Clermont, your position?'

TWR – '696Y if you hear me?'

IT537 – 'just passed CF, going for a second circuit of the stack.'

TWR – '537 hold at 50 we have a problem, ok?'

So, what caused this tragic loss, and was it related to the Basle air crash in any way? The crew began to descend over what they thought was NDB CF, when in fact, that particular beacon was more than 30 kms away! The instructor pilot in the cockpit may also have been a distraction at a critical time. The radio compass swung 180°, possibly due to a 'pirate' radio emission, or faults in the equipment on board. The cold front weather and precipitation exasperated the electrical problems affecting the ADF equipment.

<u>Lured to destruction</u>

Does any of this have any bearing upon the loss of Oscar Papa at Basle? It is exactly the same: poor weather, erroneous readings of the medium wave navigational aids, inattentive ATC because it was not really their duty to check aircraft were where they should have been. The list could go on and on. So now we can go ahead and follow all the events that led to the destruction of Oscar Papa, and also exonerate the two hapless pilots blamed, more or less, in their entirety for the accident. Let us now go through each incident that led to the fatal crash of Oscar Papa.

° approach to Basle – Rolampont to Luxeuil/Hericourt beacons. On this 10 NM wide airway, Oscar Papa flew off course to the south, 10 NMs from the centre line – in other words, 5 NMs outside the corridor. This was recorded by French military radar, hence the reason why no plot was included in the accident report. There are a couple of reasons why this deviation may have happened.

Firstly, strong winds blowing from the north at Oscar Papa's altitude; there is nothing in the report to indicate the high altitude winds – at airfield level, ATC reported between 320/8 kts – 360/10 kts, so hardly blowing an off-course gale. This was, however, from the north-west. If the wind is on the nose of an aircraft, the effects can be to slow the aircraft down. If it is on the tail, then it can speed up the aircraft.

Any other direction requires some quick calculation by the pilot to know where to point the nose of the aircraft to stay on course. I shall not go on about this as it requires a modicum of mathematical calculation, using either a hard-to-read flight computer, or pen and paper. But if the aircraft drifts off course, it will show on various cockpit instruments and the pilot knows roughly from which direction and at what speed the wind comes from – a quick calculation and turn of the nose will bring the aircraft back on course.

Thereafter, a few degrees less crabbing should help keep the aircraft on course. If the crew of Oscar Papa noticed they were outside the airway, they would surely have reported it to ATC, so that following aircraft knew of the strong winds and could take that into account. I do not believe strong wind was responsible for the deviation, otherwise ATC or the French military would have noticed and queried it?

Secondly, there could have been an error in the navigation equipment on board Oscar Papa. Remember the day before, at Luton, the ILS equipment was deviating to the left by some degree. But Oscar Papa was deviating to the right of the airway. To explain a little more we need to look briefly at the integrated flight system (IFS) that the crew would have been using at this stage of the flight.

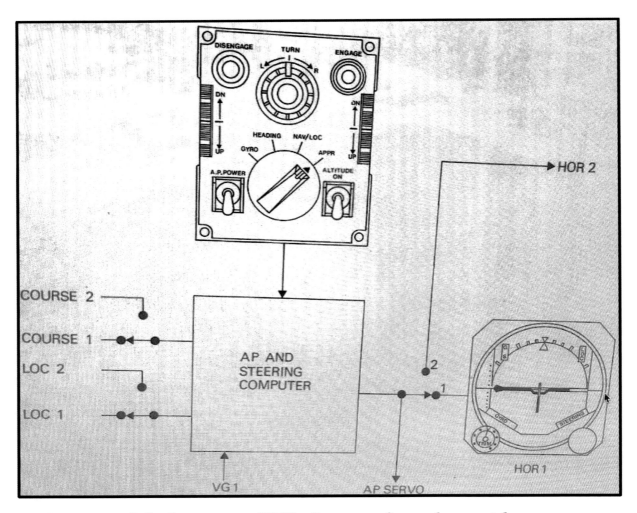

Integrated flight system (IFS) diagram from the accident report.

On the Nav1 (or 2) box, the pilot would enter the frequency of the NDB/VOR required and select a heading; by selecting 'Heading' the ADF needle (in this case) would point towards the selected NDB and, if on autopilot (A/p) the aircraft would fly direct to the beacon's overhead. If there was weather interference of the NDBs, however, the signal could be lost and the aircraft begin to drift off course. Since the deviation of Oscar Papa was back to normal tracking by Luxeuil or Hericourt, we can assume that if there was a fault with either ADF, it was only temporary and intermittent.

Thirdly, the accident report suggests the airway deviation could also be due to the crew seeking clearer weather, either to avoid turbulence or to descend in clearer weather. If this was the case, the crew would have to seek ATC permission to deviate, which they didn't, and which would have been noted by ATC, which it wasn't. Any following aircraft would be warned of turbulence ahead. The deviation, in my opinion, could only be down to recurring faults in the ADF systems, or interference due to bad weather in the vicinity of the NDB beacon transmissions the aircraft was tracking.

° approach to Bravo November NDB (BN) – a strengthening north-east wind blew a Swissair DC9 aircraft off course, which required a second attempt by its captain, Hans Theodor Tolen, to line up his aircraft with BN. He reported later 'Bravo November unreadable. Mike November unreadable. Indication sometimes pointing to different sides.' Vanguard Oscar Papa approached BN from the west.

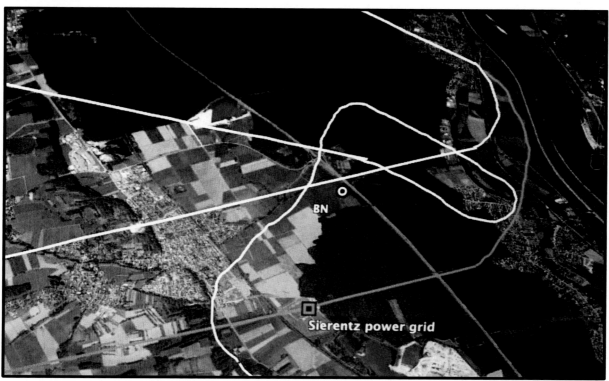

Sierentz power grid, 1 NM from BN; in all likelihood affected the ADF readings on the aircraft (red line is the new approach of Oscar Papa affected by Sierentz. White line is the accident report approach) (courtesy Google Earth)

But between Oscar Papa and BN, was the power terminal at Sierentz, with its myriad of overhead power cables not just supplying homes, but the overhead power cables of the French railway system.

The *Electricite de France* grid was transmitting messages on 306 kHz. BN was transmitting on 306.5 kHz. Because of the snowy weather and short circuits at the overhead cable line insulators, Oscar Papa's procedure over BN was begun over Sierentz power grid, instead.

A strong NE wind then blew the aircraft off course at the same time, as it did to Captain Tolen a little later. The radio magnetic compass must have swung rapidly between both signal sources as the crew of Oscar Papa fought to head out on 338° towards MN; like Tolen later, they could not detect MN since it was unreadable, and their only choice was to circle left and seek out BN again.

Normally, when crossing BN, the aircraft would continue east for about 2.2 miles, crossing the river at Basle, before turning onto 338° and heading for MN – see picture below. But because the stronger signal was from the Sierentz power station, the turn left was made before the river.

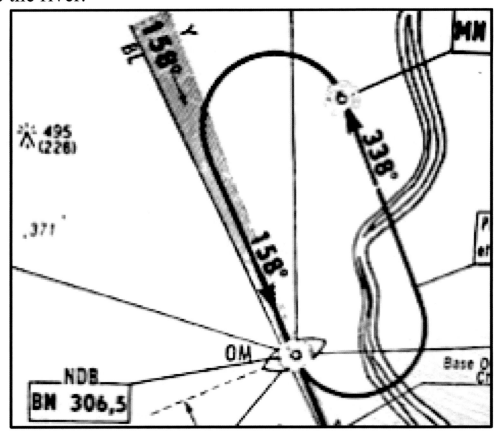

Above: fly past BN, eastbound, then cross the river before heading left onto 338° towards MN?

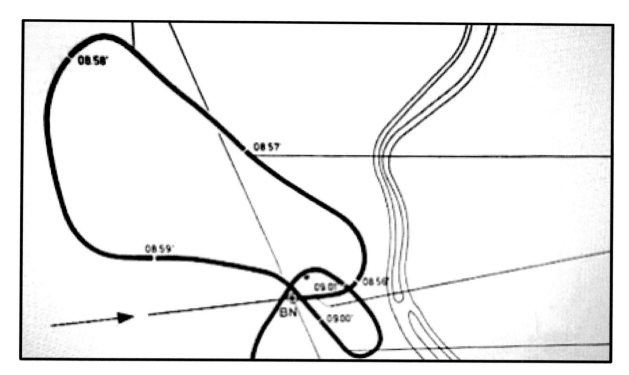

Oscar Papa never crossed the river to find MN (above both courtesy

of accident report appendix)

Because of the strong wind, the aircraft could not maintain 338° but instead headed NW. But those strong illegal signals from Sierentz broadcasting on 306 kHz swung the compass needle towards the power station. The crew most probably thought BN was left of them, so naturally turned sharply and continued south for about 3.5 NMs, when the compass needle suddenly indicated left again (for BN), because they were now closer to that beacon than the power station.

They continued to follow a course for BN, compensating for the strong NE wind before coming nice and close to the beacon – it is possible they also picked up the ILS localizer, and turned suddenly sharply to the right to intercept it. But, in all likelihood the ADF needles now swung from the BN direction to the Sierentz power station again. Evidently puzzled, the crew circled to the left once more.

° manoeuvring around BN – a short period of time now followed in which the accident report suggests the Vanguard made a sharp 180° turn, back the way it had just come, whilst deviating in altitude by 950 feet. This is the small oblong at BN on the accident report map below.

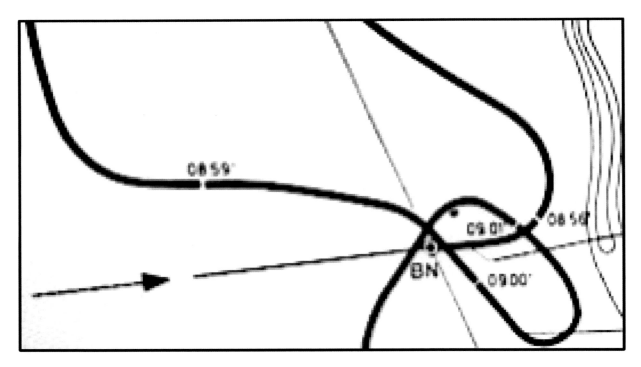

Manoeuvring around BN in a tight oblong circuit (courtesy accident report appendix)

Initially, the aircraft reported to ATC 'BN turning outbound, will call MN.' But they never called MN again, since this was unreadable and could not be found on their ADF equipment. Instead, they found themselves manoeuvring around BN and picking up the localizer beam.

The suggestion by the accident investigators that the aircraft completed this sharp 180° turn and deviation in altitude of 950 feet is frankly not very likely for a Vanguard aircraft. The likelihood is that the aircraft would breakup if it attempted such a turn with the altitude changes incurred – the aircraft is considered stable in such conditions in the landing configuration. This turn is possibly an error in interpretation of the FDR by the investigators. The aircraft now passed BN slightly to the east, at an altitude of 3200 feet instead of the assigned altitude of 1923 feet.

° first landing attempt – passing BN between transmissions from Sierentz, the aircraft picked up the localizer beam for runway 16 and proceeded south. Dorman continued his descent at just after 09:02, crossing the localizer and flying abeam the runway centreline – why did he do this? Why was he about 2 kms (1.2 NMs) left of centre?

Perhaps because the fault that manifested itself the day before at Luton had occurred again?

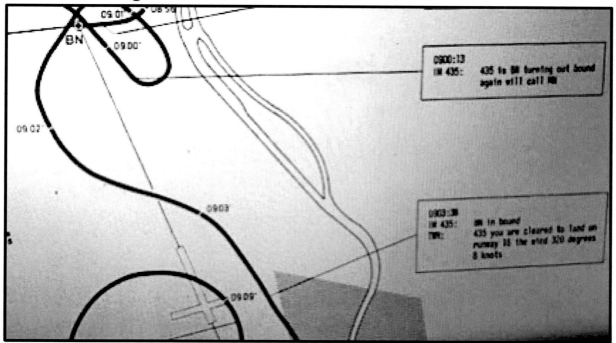

Dorman's first attempt to land – flying about 1.2 NMs left of the runway centreline, as the aircraft had done the day before at Luton (courtesy accident report appendix)

The aircraft had deviated to the left on the localizer; now it was doing it again. At the same time, the airport was below minimums for a Vanguard and the air traffic controller was sending away a French speaking crew of an Air Inter flight. But not Oscar Papa, who continued flying south-east. It entered an area of electrical interference near St Louis railway station, about a mile or so east of the Basle runway, broadcasting illegally on 306 kHz – close to the 306.5 kHz of BN. We know this was so because Terry calls passing BN inbound at this point.

This illegal transmission came from an industrial area next to the railway station. Terry's BN was a ghost transmission. The fault in the ILS equipment, notably the localizer, did not help matters, and they were noticeably left of the LOC centreline and picking up a back beam. What they were not picking up was the OM (outer marker) at BN. They passed Binningen observatory at about 09:04.40, where Mr Beck saw their red tail and made an emergency call to Basle tower. The timed distance from BN to the next maker, the MM (middle marker) was 95 seconds. When it did not sound in the cockpit, Dorman overshot and continued around to seek out BN again.

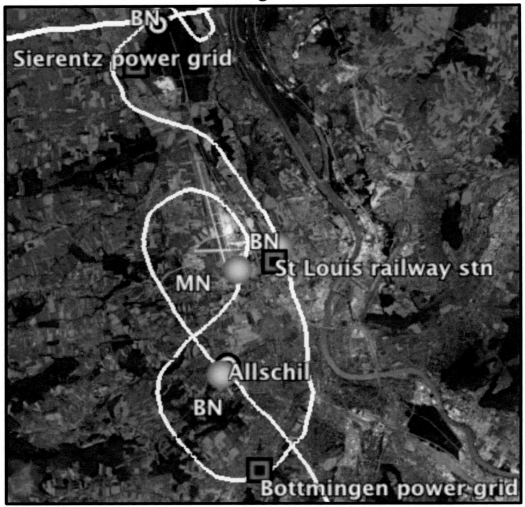

Ghost beacons (yellow) and illegal transmission sites (red) (courtesy Google Earth)

° the ghosts of BN and MN – as the Swiss accident report now says, coincident with this first overshoot was a change of radio operator on Oscar Papa, indicating a change of flying pilot. Announcing the decision to go around, air traffic seemed intrigued and radioed back '435 you are overshooting?' What he did not do was check his radar scope, which, despite a black hole over the airport, would have shown Oscar Papa about 5 NMs south of the airfield – Zurich Area Control Centre certainly picked up their echo.

On the return to BN, the aircraft passed very close to power lines at Allschil, who were also broadcasting illegally on 306 kHz – the power cables and railway surrounding Basle airport were all connected to Sierentz power station. This was another ghost of BN. But surely there was no MN available? Its signals were unreadable in the heavy snow, plus it was over 14 NMs away to the north.

Two and a half miles after passing the ghost of BN, the second compass on the Vanguard suddenly indicated MN. How was this possible? The distance between BN and MN should have been about 10 kms, or 5.4 NMs. But here it was, swinging the compass as the aircraft passed overhead. Somewhere near St Louis railway station, on the industrial estate, a factory was broadcasting illegally on 111.5 kHz.

This was traced after the accident by investigators. The third harmonic of 111.5 is 334.5 kHz (111.5 multiplied by 3). MN was set at 335.5 kHz, close enough for the compass on Oscar Papa to swing towards the illegal transmission and prompting the crew to report passing MN. As per the landing charts, they turned left and headed back towards the ghost of BN at Allschil, watching closely their ILS indicator and lining up for the centreline – again, to the left of it slightly.

° second and final attempt – Captain Terry was now flying the aircraft as they began to descend and head towards the wavering BN ghost at Allschil, which Dorman reported to ATC as simply 'BN.' They must also have been expecting the OM signal too, since this was located alongside BN; only being nowhere near it, the signal did not sound in the cockpit.

At 09:12.10 the controller, having spoken first to Mr Beck at the observatory and then the west sector controller at Zurich, suddenly came to his senses. 'Are you sure you are over BN?' he asked. 'I think've got a spurious indication – we are on the Lo…on the ILS now, sir,' replied Dorman.

'Ah!' replied ATC.

Twenty-three seconds later, slightly left of the centreline and heading close to 158° which was the runway heading, the crew reported back to ATC.

'BN is established, on localizer and glide path. The ADF's all over the place in this weather.'

Five seconds later ATC replied 'for information I don't see you on my scope radar. I don't see you on my scope radar.' Twenty-five seconds later, the controller asked for the aircraft's altitude. The final radio call from Oscar Papa came back immediately.

'One thousand four hundred on the QNH,' both pilots said together.

'Ho! I think you are on the south of the field; you are not on the… you are on the south of the field.'

Twenty-one seconds later, Oscar Papa hit the mountain.

° their final words – 'I think've got a spurious indication – we are on the Lo…on the ILS now, sir,' came from Dorman. The crew were fully aware that they were receiving spurious indications in their cockpit, and were on their guard. Because the ADF indications for BN and MN were spurious and the compass needle swinging, the crew had only the ILS and those marker beacons for additional guidance.

'We are on the Lo…on the ILS now, sir.' Confirmation that they were on localizer / glide path (ILS) meant they had lateral (LOC) as well as vertical (GS) guidance. To select ILS, the pilot has to tune in correctly to the LOC frequency 109.5 MHz and then on his instruments, such as Radio Magnetic Indicator (RMI) or Artificial Horizon (AH) or another dedicated instrument, set the ILS heading of 158°.

The glideslope doesn't need to be tuned, since it is automatically selected when LOC is tuned. So, the crew confirmed they had lateral indications (left/right of centreline) and vertical indications (2.44° slope). There was little for them to worry about too much, except for the confirmation of the OM (alongside BN), MM (0.6 NMs from runway threshold) and the IM (on the threshold). But these never came, prompting the pilots on both occasions to sensibly overshoot.

'For information I don't see you on my scope radar.' This brought no reaction from the crew, who were probably concentrating so much in landing their aircraft. Likewise, 'Ho! I think you are on the south of the field; you are not on the… you are on the south of the field.'

They had previously given their altitude of 1400 feet QNH, which was their last transmission. It is likely when the controller called about being south of the field, the crew and the passengers were hitting trees and crashing into the mountain.

8

Exonerate and remember

It is about time a book was written about the Basle tragedy, and that of the Dan Air Tenerife disaster, too. Hence my two books. Others are following. Regarding Basle, this was a complete disaster of the worst kind; so many mothers killed and children left motherless, husbands left wifeless. Even the pilots had wives and children left behind.

Relatives prepare to fly out to Basle (unknown, local press)

Shortly after the crash, relatives of the dead were flown out to Basle to help identify their loved ones. The following pictures are from the local newspapers.

Survivors return – wheelchairs on standby

Survivors return (courtesy of local press including Weston, Worle & Somerset Mercury newspaper)

Relatives depart for Basle (photos courtesy of local press)

Relatives return (photos courtesy of local press)

Further photos follow here of the crash scene and investigators working through the wreckage. Courtesy of local foreign TV news.

Blood on wreckage

This ends the story of Oscar Papa, the aircraft lured to destruction on a Swiss mountain because of the intransigence. Despite the earlier disaster at Noiretable, and warnings from the British CEGB from as early as 1969, some countries refused to stop completely sending messages via the power cables and railway overhead cables of *Electricite de France* and the French national railways.

The French dragged their feet, along with the Swiss who also paid for the operation at Basle airport, in installing a VOR beacon that would not be affected by bad weather. The head of the Swiss investigating team, Kurt Lier, was also astonished when the French allowed only two people, Gueritot and Roques, to give direct evidence at the enquiry! Harsh words were exchanged between Lier and Gueritot, and apparently the Frenchman walked out.

It was no wonder the French were being so cautious about sending representatives: the medium range NDB beacons at Basle were of the inferior A101 standard, responsible for the Noiretable crash (amongst others); ATC at Basle had given permission for Oscar Papa to land when the airfield was below minimums and other aircraft were diverting, and they had made no effort to check the progress of Oscar Papa (outside of the central blank cone radar area) until it was too late. And only then, it was upon the prompting of Mr Beck at Binningen observatory and the west sector controller at Zurich ACC.

We've seen about the message signalling between power stations using frequencies so close to that of many air traffic navigation aids. After Noiretable, several pilots contacted investigators about radio interference to navigation aids, but because they could not prove their theories at the time, they were not investigated further. It was all put down to momentary phenomena.

In June 1974, a French military aircraft with special equipment was sent to test beacons in the Belfort/Basle areas. At Belfort the aircraft was lured away from the beacon by momentary phenomena and would have likely crashed on a hill had it not been flown in clear conditions. Senior men found it incredulous that this should be so, and switched off the beacon.

Investigations continued at Basle too, where similar phenomena were observed. Investigator Jean Forestier completed his report and issued it to the French department of aeronautical navigation, the British civil aviation authority (CAA), the Swiss pilots association, the French equivalent SNLP and the British pilots union BALPA. All of this was after the Noiretable/Basle crashes, but before their respective accident reports had been published.

Despite all the obvious findings by Forestier regarding the phenomena, not one word relating to it appears in the Basle accident report, and it's only mentioned briefly, as some momentary phenomena, in Noiretable. Although this report was available for the senior Basle investigators, none of them spoke to Forestier or any of the electricity generating companies. The report did, however, have one effect – *Electricite de France* switched off their 306 kHz transmissions.

Another omission from the report was the exclusion of eight other pilots who submitted reports that day confirming that the BN/MN signals were unreadable, or that there was a strong NE wind blowing them off course. How did these pilots, some of whom diverted, get around the unreadable BN/MN signals, and why was it that the crew of Oscar Papa didn't?

The other crews were all jet pilots, flying faster and higher aircraft than the slow moving Vanguard. The jet crews approaching Basle had a better 'line of sight' for alternative navigational aids that Oscar Papa did not. The most obvious ones were Luxeuil VOR, 50 NMs west, and Hochwald VOR 9 NMs to the south, but for both mountains stood in the way of low flying aircraft like Oscar Papa.

Since the French ministry of posts and telecommunications (with its subsidiary radio and electricity services) were responsible for granting the licenses and approving the frequencies for use in transmitting messages, this I believe explains why the French were reluctant to be fully represented at the enquiry. This is hardly surprising, considering their intransigence led to the deaths of 108 people on a Swiss mountain, and 60 more people on a French hillside.

INDEX

Made in the USA
Middletown, DE
04 April 2021